TAROT GOTHICA

JANNE KOIVUNIEMI

Schiffer Publishing Ltd

4880 Lower Valley Road • Atglen, PA 19310

TAROT GOTHICA

JANNE KOIVUNIEMI

Copyright © 2015 by Janne Koivuniemi

Library of Congress Control Number: 2014956474

All rights reserved. No part of this work may be reproduced or used in any form or by any means—graphic, electronic, or mechanical, including photocopying or information storage and retrieval systems—without written permission from the publisher.

The scanning, uploading, and distribution of this book or any part thereof via the Internet or via any other means without the permission of the publisher is illegal and punishable by law. Please purchase only authorized editions and do not participate in or encourage the electronic piracy of copyrighted materials. "Schiffer," "Schiffer Publishing, Ltd. & Design," and the "Design of pen and inkwell" are registered trademarks of Schiffer Publishing, Ltd.

Type set in Crown Title/Bodoni MT/Minion Pro

ISBN: 978-0-7643-4818-1

Printed in China

Published by
Schiffer Publishing, Ltd.
4880 Lower Valley Road
Atglen, PA 19310
Phone: (610) 593-1777
Fax: (610) 593-2002
E-mail: Info@schifferbooks.com

For our complete selection of fine books on this and related subjects, please visit our website at www.schifferbooks.com. You may also write for a free catalog.

This book may be purchased from the publisher. Please try your bookstore first.

We are always looking for people to write books on new and related subjects. If you have an idea for a book, please contact us at proposals@schifferbooks.com.

Schiffer Publishing's titles are available at special discounts for bulk purchases for sales promotions or premiums. Special editions, including personalized covers, corporate imprints, and excerpts can be created in large quantities for special needs. For more information, contact the publisher.

These cards are dedicated to all my beautiful models, and secrets they reveal.

Special thanks to
Laura Pihlaja and Terhi Virkki

TABLE OF

Preface	8	**The Arcana Minor**	33
		BATONS	**34**
The Arcana Major	**10**	Ace of Batons	35
0–The Fool	11	2 of Batons	35
1–The Magician	12	3 of Batons	36
2–The High Priestess	13	4 of Batons	36
3–The Empress	14	5 of Batons	37
4–The Emperor	15	6 of Batons	38
5–The High Priest	16	7 of Batons	38
6–The Lovers	17	8 of Batons	39
7–The Chariot	18	9 of Batons	39
8–Justice	19	10 of Batons	40
9–The Hermit	20	Princess of Batons	41
10–Destiny	21	Prince of Batons	42
11–Strength	22	Queen of Batons	43
12–Hanged	23	King of Batons	44
13–Death	24		
14–Temperance	25	**CHALISES**	**45**
15–The Devil	26	Ace of Chalises	46
16–The Tower	27	2 of Chalises	46
17–The Star	28	3 of Chalises	47
18–The Moon	29	4 of Chalises	47
19–The Sun	30	5 of Chalises	48
20–Judgment	31	6 of Chalises	48
21–The World	32		

CONTENTS

7 of Chalises	49
8 of Chalises	50
9 of Chalises	50
10 of Chalises	51
Princess of Chalises	52
Prince of Chalises	53
Queen of Chalises	54
King of Chalises	55
SWORDS	**56**
Ace of Swords	57
2 of Swords	57
3 of Swords	58
4 of Swords	58
5 of Swords	59
6 of Swords	59
7 of Swords	60
8 of Swords	61
9 of Swords	62
10 of Swords	63
Princess of Swords	64
Prince of Swords	65
Queen of Swords	66
King of Swords	67

COINS	**68**
Ace of Coins	69
2 of Coins	69
3 of Coins	70
4 of Coins	70
5 of Coins	71
6 of Coins	71
7 of Coins	72
8 of Coins	72
9 of Coins	73
10 of Coins	73
Princess of Coins	74
Prince of Coins	75
Queen of Coins	76
King of Coins	77
Conclusion	**78**

PREFACE

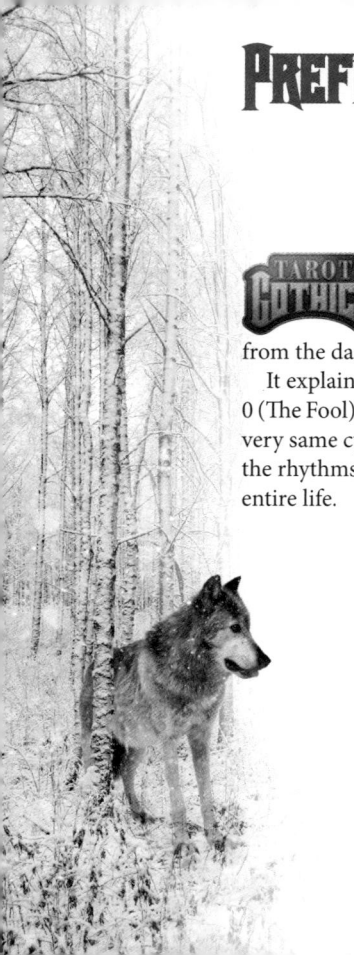

TAROT GOTHICA shows the way from the light to the lighter and from the dark to the darker.

It explains the circle of life from card 0 (The Fool) to card 21 (The World). The very same cycle can be found hidden in the rhythms of each day, a year, or one's entire life.

Tarot's rhythm is similar to nature's: if one is able to listen to his/her inner feelings, one may notice things to occur in a certain order.

If preferred, cards may be read through the symbolic pictures, like a book. Or you can draw three cards from the pack to see the quality of the past, this moment, and the future. Any way you are willing to proceed, each card has to be lived *through*.

Let these cards be your advice.

0—The Fool

To whom belongs the one who
   does not belong?
Ignoring trouble.
Looking above where the light
   shall end.
Trusting in itself.
Following one's own path towards
   highness, towards Light.

One's true, free self. Sails in a stream of life. Gazing to the light at the end of a narrow path. The way of the initiate. The carrier of the scythe has the ability to use it. Half a man, half a dog, as a memory of the lower path—slowing down and guarding old habits, clinging to worldliness. As the time goes, the animal side will be left behind. You have the choice to let the animal bite what is left of you, still following the burden of the past—or, let go and keep following the path leading to the Light.

Advice: The future is in your own hands; everything you see is a new chance.

1—The Magician

Seeing the strangest things with
   one's own eyes.
The ability to believe or deny.
Only The Magician knows
   the secret.
There is no difference between
   black and white.
The force remains the same for all.

The strong Magician knows both sides of the force without drawing lines between the two. With head in the clouds, feet on the earth, and mastering oneself, The Magician remains balanced. There is power; there is wisdom. With them, one can both build or destroy.

Advice: Think of your motives; everything you need is within you. Seek your purpose.

2—The High Priestess

The route behind the mind.
The rhythm of existence.
Mastered ecstasy lifts the soul high, giving way for the Light to land in your soul.
From higher, you will see the entirety into which the shadow of yourself does not reach.

Intuition, high knowledge. The High Priestess finds the way into greater consciousness. Drumming divides the balance, making one able to see the good and evil at the same moment. The rhythm echoes in ancient temples, bringing wisdom to the ruler. She can only hear it when completely open, not betrayed within herself.

Advice: Trust in your inner balance, let it bring up your wisdom. Unless you remain in rhythm, that same rhythm will beat you down. Find your rhythm of life, loud voice of silence, and your inner voice.

3—The Empress

Beauty, inside and out, makes the land flourish.
Full of tenderness, sometimes cruel, a tool to unite heaven and earth.

The knife divides justice and protects from harm. The skulls of the ancestresses remind one of the call of the earth and the continuing circle of life. The higher wisdom keeps the land fertile. The divine beauty itself is reason enough to justify the ruler. Creative force, in harmony with worldly matters… Let it flow fairly and enjoy, or the next Empress shall hold your skull.

Advice: As you sow, so shall you reap. Think! You will carry all consequences.

4—The Emperor

Power is gained only by demanding it.
Only the death of the king will give room for the new Emperor.

The ambitious, strong ruler. The one who sees and leads the way, the absolute authority. Skulls of ancestors remind one of wisdom and all things worldly. The sword is resting, but ready to make the difference between what is forbidden and what is allowed. Whoever stands in his way will turn to dust... Power is followed by growth and flourishing and, on the other hand, death and destruction. They are inseparable.
Which one do you see? The choice is yours.

Advice: You have power to change the world that you see. You will affect the lives of others, too—be wise.

5—The High Priest

Priest takes the death away from the days of the living, according to the ritual and learned morale. Birth, Life, Death, and the one without the name—not one is weaker than the other.

The High Priest holds the truth and teaches it only if one can hear. The dogma is not for everyone; one may get lost in it. Fire is seen to all, but the flame is unknown. Does the fiery rod of The Priest speak of the new beginning? The dogma is not the same for the wizard and the plain folk. Knowledge is available. It may lead to dogma, the death of the true faith or, it may give the tools to become free, to be reborn mentally.

Advice: You will start to see behind everyday routines. You may still repeat them as usual, but the motive is different.

6—The Lovers

Spring arrives in the midst of winter
  without conditions or prejudices.
The wings of love will carry.
The power of life,
  overwhelming, agreeable.

Perfect understanding, complete balance, union between man, heaven, and earth. Coldness will disappear, the power brings all things beautiful into sight and, in the eyes of love, everything is fair. The power of life, like the eternal moment just before the first kiss. You do not possess love. Let it flow within or you will soon be but a cold ruin where the wind blows the dust of memories on your grave. Love is strong. It causes life—and death.

Advice: Will you go with your heart or mind? You must find the way for them to serve the same purpose.

7—The Chariot

The chariot of human lions rushes on, driven by the demons of their consciousness.
Action without a thought, without a doubt, not questioning a single thing, goes ahead according to the driver's will.
A perfect tool.

The Chariot has been tamed to function as the driver pleases. It keeps going when she wants and stops when she says. This demon cannot be stopped by anyone but herself. The rage of the driver's demon can be heard in the roar of human lions.

Advice: The change is near. Accept it! You have the tools to carry on in great glory; just take care of the right direction.

8—Justice

For justice to be done for everyone,
may the most powerful of
forces, Love and Death,
stay inseparable forever.

Life and death in the scales, the halves of existence balanced by the sword of truth. Massive rocks as the basis, hot and cold in the background, light and dark, the undistributed halves of the same things. The balance of opposites and the realization of unity is a truth where higher understanding may be fulfilled. Imbalance and destruction are a result of using force.

Advice: This is your chance to be truthful to yourself. Without it, you cannot understand others.

9—The Hermit

Winter lives in a soul, peace
   in a white landscape.
Away from the world,
   alone in loneliness.
The beast does not see the
   difference between itself
   and others.
Beauty as cruel as a fairy tale.

Isolated from the world and its influences. On a journey to oneself, without interruption, as a student of nature, with the beasts... It is time to concentrate on all that is true and essential. The road to silence is found from inside; turn there. This route is well hidden and lonely.

Advice: Search in silence and travel slow, otherwise you'll turn into a beast. Man is a wolf to another man.

10—Destiny

Though you may fly on the wings of Seraph—two carry you into the heights, four shield you from the brightness—you cannot escape destiny.
It follows the departing and awaits the arrival, traveling by your side on the journey.
Stare straight into its eyes, it may be kinder than you think.

Faith, the initial force, creates all that exists. It is the reason and the cause—the absolute law in the universe. We are its children, rulers, and slaves. It can be seen in the four elements: fire, wind, water, and earth. The cycle has closed. Follow the river, even if you cannot see the cause. If you go against the flow, it will kill your strength.

Advice: Go with strength and intuition. By choosing well, you may get rid of old Karma.

11—Strength

Slowly grown over the years.
Spiritual power, true nobility
 forgives his own murder.
Fear refined into Power; the Power
 to slay its final weaknesses.
The Power to die along with
 its weaknesses.

Strength is seen from afar. It glows with passion and creativity. No matter how big the obstacle, the inner power will even rise above itself. The dragon will no longer burn the soul with its desires: its spirit has evolved into a knight's sword of justice. It is good to get drunk of power and passion—that will create new things and lift one up. Beware, though, not to hide bad consciousness with it, otherwise the dragon will rise again, this time to destroy you. You are on the edge, you have defeated yourself. Fire still burns above the one who has failed.

Advice: Victory over yourself. Do not give hatred; take the power over your strength or you will find yourself back where you started.

12—Hanged

Fill the standards of your flock,
  commit to your tether, rope
  your leg, conform to the mold
  assigned to you, a part of
  the eternal puzzle known
  as community.
Nothing here can wildly run riot,
  if one wants to belong.

One cannot continue back or forth. Old dead tree, the one you once took good care of, has a hold on you and you don't even know whether you wish it to let go or not. It is hard to give up on the past if one cannot look forward, because of images that are already gone.

Advice: You are stuck, can't seem to escape. On the other hand, a whole new point of view opens up in front of you.

THE ARCANA MAJOR

13—Death

The time of emptiness.
The night's desolation.
The silence of morning.
The passing thought of yesterday.
No future, no past, only the present.
Only the wind crosses the land that
  no longer knows its trekker.
The bird's beak holds a reminder
  of the future.

Balance is unnecessary; nature has taken control. Scythe has done its work, separating life and death, temporal and eternal. The body will be given to the earth that once led it into being. The raven will carry life to its next form. The black figure slides over the empty ground and will find you every time, which is the only comfort there is. Life does not vanish, but the change is necessary.

Advice: This is the end of an era. Like it or not, chances will appear. Clear your mind; new things will fill you.

14—Temperance

Anger and joy, innocence and shame.
Patience and aggression, moderation and greed.
Wait a moment, tranquility brings balance, opens the beauty of the naked soul.

Nothing more is needed. Understanding the wholeness of the opposites will bring balance. When naked and innocent, one can take control over the storm inside. The center of balance, the happy median, steadily keeps the changing figures of emotional turbulence behind, although your reflection may be interpreted otherwise. Inner peace gives an opportunity to study Darkness and Light as one and enables you to make the right choices.

Advice: Accept different sides, good and bad; they do not go separately. Watch out for overkill, it may lead back to the fire.

15—The Devil

Bloodless skin, a proud glance,
one cannot bathe in light in the
house belonging to evil.
The wings don't carry you to the
heights, give a new change to
their grim possessor.

The Devil does not bow. She is proud, strong, sexual, charismatic. The animal essence is the best friend and a servant. Man will slowly be burnt to dust and the soul is released without any worth. Wings do not carry; they are but a memory of distant times that burned away, giving way to The Devil. Courage means looking at things as they are. The fear of loss has been left behind.

Advice: Now you know the Dark side, too. Without it, you would not see the Light. Using this power only for your own good will give you nothing more.

16—The Tower

Even the strongest Tower will sometimes succumb underneath a stronger force.
In the force of inevitable doom the strongest don't survive
but those who adapt.
It's time to flee and time to shelter oneself, and once again time to rebuild.

The Tower has been built of matter, possession, images, and feelings of safety. It is old and worn and has become so attached to the way you think that it's hard to see something else instead. The Tower is a learned formula or order that has turned into a dogma. Balance lies in the ground, fallen; hopes and images will turn to illusion—the truth tearing them apart. Great change—that might have been foreseen, but not recognized—will come with the same bold force as the changes in nature. May you not stay lying in the ruins—get up; it might save your soul.

Advice: Mental images are crashing to ground. Learn to live in the moment; it's all you need.

17—The Star

One of billions is that which I sanctify to myself.
From body and soul, a temple I build, of the most precious that I own.
An ancient light began its journey at the dawn of time. Its source impossible to ever reach.

The infinite energy flows through the human temple, bursting life and creativity, making everything beautiful and fertile. Lucifer, ancient force that cannot be owned, flows as an inspiration, lifting up all that it touches.

Advice: The initial force flows again, for all unnecessary structures have vanished. Let it flow in you, or you will soon be just a distant, sore shell.

18—The Moon

Ancient backdrop of the night,
  pallid reflection of the Light.
Seen by all, but its dark side
  known to none.
A secret no one notices,
  visible to all.

The Moon is feminine, secret, and intuitive. Its pale, dreamlike, beautiful skin is decorated with secrets that only those aware of their subconsciousness are able to interpret. Everyone knows that The Secret lies inside them, feels mystical things, and would like to know more, but cannot unveil the curtain of secrets. The world of mysteries is mixed with the daytime consciousness in dreams and things that are hard to explain. It is hard to separate imagination from reality. Ideas and inspiration might well be the combination of two worlds.

Advice: In Darkness, walk as in the Light: the mystical side may open a whole new world in front of you. Denying it might cause it to disappear forever.

19—The Sun

Giver and taker of life.
Neither good nor evil—just is.
With this, you do not argue.

The Sun is a boundless power of life that gives its Light to shine upon all, without limitations, without judgment. Its influence can be seen everywhere, both in matter and spirit, as force untouchable. The Sun brings joy and life, but is able to burn these things away, too. It does not know right from wrong. It is the same to everybody.

Advice: Light also brings shades. You have to know them both, or the other will destroy you.

20—Judgment

It is not a question of will I die,
  but how I die.
From the furnace of the deep
  arises a sea of hands
  struggling in the fire.

Can you still remember the time of innocence, those shining stairs of Light that once rose to that same heaven...The angel of judgment gathers up all who still have burdens to carry. It is time to make a decision, confess the last sin, pay the last Karma. Nothing will stay hidden; the fiery sword is about to burn the truth out.

Advice: The Judgment is absolute. Finish whatever is still in progress! Without this atonement, you cannot be free; find the road ahead.

21—The World

Melodies, orbits, fractals.
From the micro-cosmos to the multi-universe they follow the order of chaos.
They beat with the rhythm of Light from nonexistent to the existing.

Life giver of the universe, Mother God, the power at the edge of being and nonexistent, creates the matter with her voice. Gives to energy its rhythm, nature's laws their melody... She has created everything, her breath is the same as ours. The path has led to a higher level: The Fool has become The Master; the goal has been reached. Keep going, keep creating with the universe, be a part of the great instrument.

Advice: Find the harmony, for nature will fix all your broken parts.

THE ARCANA MINOR

BATONS

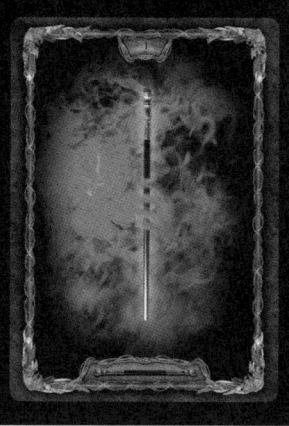 

Ace of Batons

Fire: the element of batons

Creativity, intuition, and burning passion awakening, old energy works without any regard to limits, as in nature.

The initial force of Masculinity.

2 of Batons

Consideration

The power of flame has been awakened—consider how you use it.

You are able to receive new energy, think of its beginning and purpose so you can control it.

3 of Batons

Authority

A well-balanced position that awaits the implementation of action.

No conflict in sight; your inner fire reflects in the eyes of others.

4 of Batons

Celebration

Happiness and content flows through everyone.

Something has reached completion or a new one begins.

There is reason to celebrate and rejoice.

5 of Batons

The Call

Challenges to face, withheld energy, your own Angels and Demons.

Something has been forgotten in the back of your mind, and the time to face it has now come.

Find the edge of your darkness.

6 of Batons

Victory

Victory has been achieved, as if it were the most simple thing in the world.

A long road and firm confidence have made the goal a reality.

7 of Batons

Adversity

Ideas are resisted.

Resistance causes defensiveness and it may lead you deeper to the matter.

8 of Batons

Action

Things move fast
and impulsively.

Quick decisions and
events, focused energy, and
sparking erotic vortexes.

9 of Batons

Uncertainty

Uncertain confidence
makes you doubt.

There is energy, but it is
being restrained; there is no
certain path and you don't
dare to show
your resources.

10 of Batons

Suffocation

The fire has been smothered and has been accumulated into a burden.

Things are locked in and life does not flow naturally.

What was once interesting, now seems boring and things run in circles.

Princess of Batons

Creator and destroyer

Fearless and uninhibited.

Young as spring, unprejudiced, and activity is sparked.

Fresh, innocent force brings forth much new.
Works here and now.

Prince of Batons

The messenger, who is often unexpected

An appealing force who does not care about the recipient's expectations.

Tidings from things to come.

Queen of Batons

A strong, attractive healer

Warm and understanding.

A character conscious of her power and charisma, both spiritually and erotically; joy of life and experience bring admirers from near and far.

King of Batons

A charismatic protagonist,
who combines knowledge and skills

The creative force that connects spirit and matter, fire and iron, and knows how this will benefit all.

Ace of Chalises

Water: the element of chalises

Strong, pure feelings, love.

The cleansing of things, wisdom in feelings.

2 of Chalises

Unity

Connection and sexuality, the merging together of lovers.

The passionate harmony of two halves to which the judgment of others has no effect.

3 of Chalises

Relationships

Togetherness and strong friendship; joy and the sharing of feelings.

Blood is thicker than water.

4 of Chalises

Closure

Loss of motivation.

Turned inwards, the paused mind wants to distance itself from things.

5 of Chalises

Grief

Fear of loss and disappointment.

You feel only grief and can see nothing else until the last tear has fallen.

6 of Chalises

Pleasure

The free rush of sensuality in both small and great things.

Sincere eroticism, harmonic fulfillment.

7 of Chalises

Dreams

Dreams are picked from the stream of sleep and they guide the direction of desires.

Dreams are strong influences and may bring about great things, but without strong direction of will, only dreams they remain. Recognize the lines of your dreams in daily life and try to look further: Where can they take you?

8 of Chalises

Surrender

Turn your back on the old, and travel towards a new time.

You cannot see the new, if you are full of the old.

9 of Chalises

Satisfaction

Strong confidence and happiness.

A strong nature will bring before you all that you require.

10 of Chalises

Fulfillment

Togetherness and happiness are achieved.

Emotions flow exuberantly into things that you have reached for and there is no threat.

Princess of Chalises

Freedom and youth

The ability to enjoy life without restraint.

The sensitivity to succumb to spiritual things, creative intuition, and beauty.

Prince of Chalises

The ability to quickly respond to situations

An independent, noble, romantic character that is prudent, open and, if needed, actively functional.

Queen of Chalises

The inner feminine side

Mistress who answers for dreams and reality.

Travels between two worlds, guided by love and passion, causing feelings to become action.

King of Chalises

Force of the subconscious

Spiritual light in the darkness of matter leads to the courage to be just.

Mastering art, science, and emotion in a chopping sea of desire.

SWORDS

SWORDS

Ace of Swords

Air: the element of swords

Will, truth, and justice.

Sharp detection
and resolution.

Clear understanding and
purpose with no need
for compromises.

2 of Swords

Delicate balance

Inward withdrawal
and contemplation.

The mind is in a fragile
state searching for Darkness
in Light and Light from
Darkness. The inner world,
untouched by the
outer world.

3 of Swords

Heartbreak

Inner turmoil.

Conflicts and a painful truth coming forward, traveling through emotional tempests, such as joys—also, sorrow is beautiful.

4 of Swords

Stagnation

Withdrawing into timelessness.

A standstill where you may be cleansed of the burden.

A calming place, with silence, though you still hear the fury of the storm.

5 of Swords

Defeat

You have been defeated.

Humiliation or loss that will only intensify if you fight it and don't swallow your pride.

6 of Swords

Insight

The understanding of the fallen leads to a new beginning.

The Fallen Angel remembers the long forgotten beauty in the flower she just picked and sees all with new eyes.

7 of Swords

Frustration

The Light and Dark both attract, but neither offer the truth.

Thoughtless acts. Temptation to take unnecessary action ordered by cravings.

The spirit won't rise to see behind the fog.

8 of Swords

Bewilderment

An apparent conflict.

A confusing situation, trapped with no solution in sight, even if the problem were gone.

If only you'd lift your gaze and turn to take a look.

9 of Swords

Horror

The "Dreamworld" brings darkness to your mind.

The dark side of the past aims to come forth and crawl into your consciousness through dreams, until you recognize that it is all part of you. Both higher feelings and lower thoughts, everything you can experience, are what you are made of.

10 of Swords

Menace

Dreaded things come flooding in.

The struggle is in vain; boundaries are broken and all you can do is give in to the storm.

A turning point, with no going back.

King of Swords

Charismatic power and wisdom

The ability to deal out justice without limitations.

Masculine creativity and relentlessness, responsible for decisions.

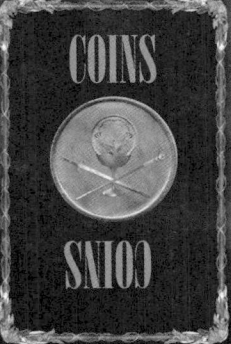

Ace of Coins

Earth: the element of coins

Wealth and well being.

To succeed financially and spiritually.

2 of Coins

Balance

Security of wealth and good fortune.

The balancing of opposites.

3 of Coins

Creativity and skill

Creativity brings spirit and skill, the tools to professionally carry out plans into masterpieces.

4 of Coins

Taking care of

You take care of your own and you can no longer see to the outside of things.

You only see dangers that you wish to avoid.

5 of Coins

Misfortunes

Things won't let go, they pull you into darkness. Trouble and misfortune...

Let it be; it'll only get worse.

6 of Coins

Sharing

Righteous generosity brings about a balanced Karma.

Donation creates circulation that returns.

7 of Coins

Patience

Patient waiting and trust in the future will in time bring prey, though you may not see it now.

8 of Coins

Know-how

Diligence and know-how in work.

Determination in professional activities.

9 of Coins

Success

Work has brought about result, serenity, and contentment.

Time of harvest.

10 of Coins

Family

Achievements in work make it possible to focus on family, friends, and the solidarity of close relatives.

Princess of Coins

Fulfilling ideas in practice

Worldly and spiritual ladders lead upwards.

Prince of Coins

Clear goal

Worldly things are in order and your gaze is focused on the gate of spiritual horizon.

Queen of Coins

A free, strong leader who knows his/her place

Feet firmly on rock and the clarity to see the other side of the spiritual barrier.

King of Coins

The financial and spiritual opinion-maker

A strong character with the wealth and charisma to realize his authority.

CONCLUSION

When mind openly reaches its night side, colors and shapes appear stronger. Different tones of light are glowing new and strange in embrace velvet of darkness. No difference in Light and Darkness, only ensemble, when the darker side accepts itself.

Beauty is power hidden in everything, even in sorrow and death, which are usually closed off from one's mind. There is a timeless, temperate strength, a wordless sense of raw beauty.

So, as you take this path, there is no turning back; you will feel happiness and sorrow. Step inside your emotions; there is a chance to grow beyond limits.